# SECTIONS

# HOW TO USE THIS JOURNAL

YOUR JOURNAL. YOUR WAY.

Record, solve, clarify, re-frame and explore your inner world, to get to know yourself and empower yourself, so you can create a life you love, doing it your way.

We've included explorative, thought provoking activities to help you uncover your values, motivators, and your impact, so you can extract the most joy and happiness from your life.

One of the secrets to happiness and fulfilment for women comes from helping people through our own ways of doing that, so you'll notice this is encouraged as a daily practice, along with reflection and gratitude.

To support your emotional development for personal growth, we've included the best reframing exercises as tools. These help you see alternative perspectives that shift your thinking and emotions as needed, so life lessons are more easily adopted.

You are stronger than you know, but in life's testing moments in doesn't feel like that because the intensity of our emotions can block us from making quality decisions, so we've included a whole section on Emotional and Mental First Aid exercises to help you in those times.

Here's to your quality, empowered life!

Enjoy your Self Empowerment Journal & Workbook.

Only you get to live your life, you may as well make the most of it!

# SECTION 1:
# YOUR PERSONAL
# EMPOWERMENT
# WORKBOOK

Prioritise your time to align with your values for a full life with meaning and deep satisfaction.

## INSTRUCTIONS:

1. Ask yourself this question, "What's TRULY important to ME?" (Exclude writing down 'things' or 'specific' people's names). Values examples can be: Friendships, Achieving, Bettering my best, Family, Respect, loyalty, adventure etc.
2. Repeat asking yourself this question at least 5 times, emptying out each time until you can't think of anymore.
3. Then on the next 2 pages you'll rank them in order of importance. This can be the most powerful exercise you ever do, because too often we waste our life on what's unimportant to us, not realising we were prioritising to what we're supposed to value, rather than what we really do.. This can lead to a life of regret, when it's too late to change it.

*"What's truly important to me?"*

Notes:
_____
_____
_____
_____
_____
_____
_____
_____
_____
_____
_____
_____
_____
_____
_____
_____
_____
_____

# MY VALUES PRIORITISED

*"If you could have only one of your values, which would it be?"*
(repeat x 10)

1. Value _____

Why? _____

_____

_____

_____

2. Value _____

Why? _____

_____

_____

_____

3. Value _____

Why? _____

_____

_____

_____

4. Value _____

Why? _____

_____

_____

_____

5. Value _____

Why? _____

_____

_____

_____

# MY VALUES PRIORITISED

1. Value _____

Why? _____

_____

_____

_____

2. Value _____

Why? _____

_____

_____

_____

3. Value _____

Why? _____

_____

_____

_____

4. Value _____

Why? _____

_____

_____

_____

5. Value _____

Why? _____

_____

_____

_____

To lead a more fulfilling life, allocate your focus and select activities
that align with your personal set of values.

# A F F I R M A T I O N S

You are unique and special, just the way you are.

You are worthy of love and respect.

You embrace your flaws and imperfections, as they make you who you are.

You are confident in your abilities and believe in your potential.

You are beautiful inside and out.

You are strong and capable of overcoming any challenge.

You are enough, just as you are.

You are surrounded by people who appreciate and value you.

You are proud of your accomplishments, big or small.

You are deserving of self-care and taking time for yourself.

You are intelligent and have the power to learn and grow.

You are worthy of setting boundaries and saying no when necessary.

You are resilient and can bounce back from setbacks.

You are capable of achieving your dreams and goals.

You are unique and have something valuable to offer the world.

# "I AM ..." versus "YOU ARE ..." Affirmations?!

'I am' affirmations are more powerful if referring to yourself without looking in a mirror, or, without seeing an image of yourself in your minds eye when saying them, otherwise, if you want them to be well adopted, they should start with 'You are' to the version of 'you', that you're saying it to. Try looking into the pits of your pupils in the mirror and addressing yourself by your name for profound results. CREATE YOUR OWN.

Eg. "You are a beautiful soul [your name] and deserve to be respected"

_____

_____

_____

_____

_____

_____

_____

_____

_____

_____

_____

_____

_____

_____

_____

_____

_____

_____

_____

# I would like to grow, improve and commit to working on ...

_____

_____

_____

_____

_____

_____

_____

_____

_____

_____

_____

_____

_____

_____

_____

_____

_____

_____

_____

_____

_____

_____

_____

# Your Ripple Impact - Visualised

Make a list of every person who has EVER thanked you for the impact you had in their life, big AND small. Then see yourself through their eyes at that moment as they did, and imagine how it felt for them, thanking you.

_____

_____

_____

_____

_____

_____

_____

_____

_____

_____

_____

_____

_____

_____

_____

_____

_____

_____

_____

_____

_____

_____

_____

_____

_____

# Your Ripple Impact - Acknowledged

What words did they say to express their appreciation? Write what they said.
(Read at least monthly or when you need to remember you're awesome!

_____
_____
_____
_____
_____
_____
_____
_____
_____
_____
_____
_____
_____
_____
_____
_____
_____
_____
_____
_____
_____
_____
_____
_____
_____
_____
_____

# Your Ripple Impact - Felt

In the puzzle pieces below, write down how this made you FEEL.
Notice how it fills all the holes within you?

This is the definition of full-fill-ment. Take a moment now to self appreciate.

# Your Ripple Impact - Reflected

- FIRST INNER RIPPLE: Write the names of those people you've DIRECTLY Impacted
- SECOND RIPPLE: List the names of people who THESE people had an impact on.
- THIRD RIPPLE: Write the names (or groups) of the people that these people Impact.

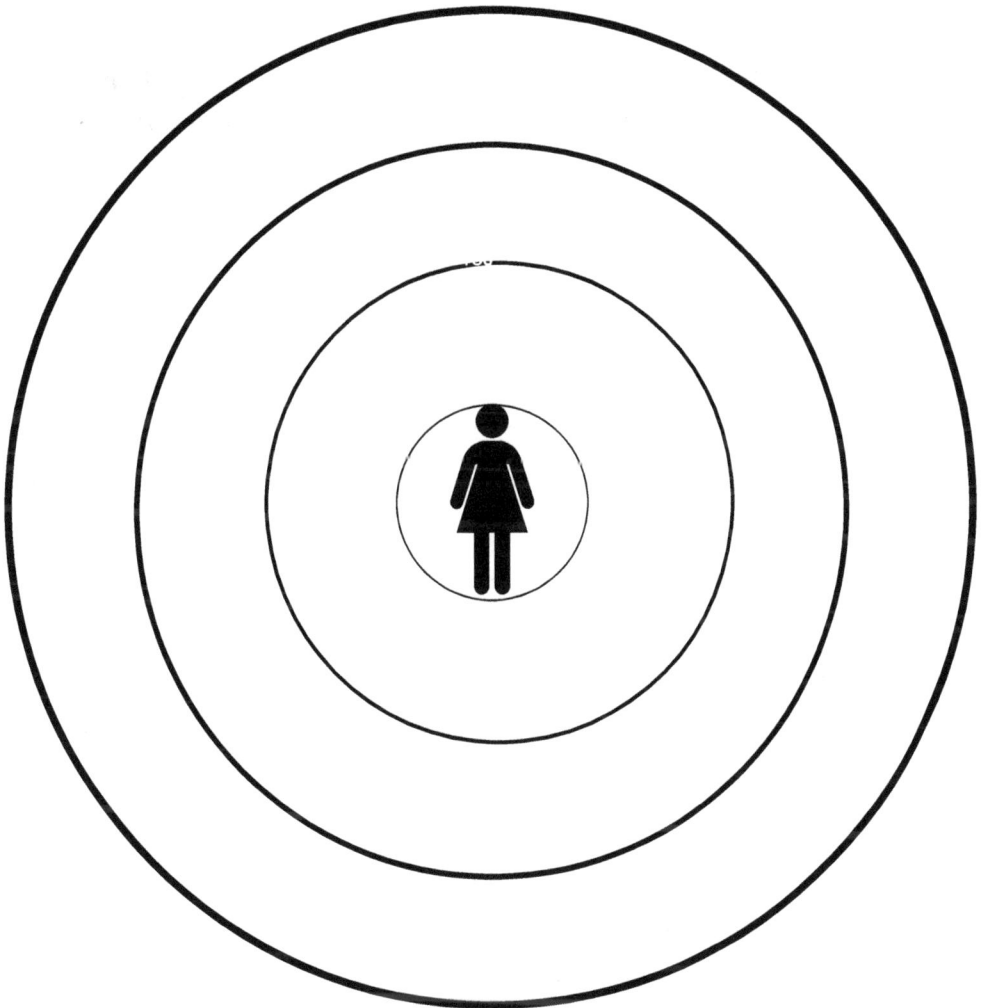

# Your Ripple Impact - Potentialised

They say we each come in direct contact with approx 8000+ people in our lifetime.

If each of those 8000 people impacted 8000 people, and those 8000 people impacted ANOTHER 8000 people - IMAGINE the difference that can be made, by YOU, simply for being you, activating your potentiality!

In your minds eye, see the Ripple Impact that YOU have already created, simply by being you and imagine if every day you positively made a difference to one person...

Could ACTUALISING your potential create a far greater ripple effect than your mind is conditioned and programmed to currently imagine? YOU BET it is absolutely possible!

_____

_____

_____

_____

_____

_____

_____

_____

_____

_____

_____

_____

_____

_____

_____

_____

_____

# You're NOT Crazy because you're female! You're a powerful Creator of life itself, and that's powHERful!

Being born female, means you are nature in human form, synced with the moon in ways beyond our knowledge. That's pow-her-ful!

Is it time to accept, appreciate and love your design as being part of you? Being wired maternally means you come packaged with an immeasurable capacity to love. This gift, while easily under-valued, (even by ourself), becomes limitless when first given to ourselves.

The more you get this, the more you accept yourself and only when you accept yourself can you love yourself, as you are.

Your ideal life creation, can begin with you.

# BIOLOGICALLY OUR FEMALENESS
(not femininity)

requires that our brain & body use
minimal power at certain times each month,
because our inner human creator generator needs
to do what it's made for.

## LET IT!

Don't fight your own nature

# I like myself because ...

Make a list of all the things that you like about yourself. Big things, and little things - they all count! Keep adding to this as new things come to mind. Write it like this: "Today, DATE, I like this about myself...."

*eg: Today I like that I'm a good listener and openly show people that I care*

# My Dreams to Make Happen

Use this space to list down the things that you would like to accomplish or experience. It's always great to dream or have a vision of something to look forward to or make happen. Don't worry that you don't think you can yet, but you'll be surprised at how writing these down, end up becoming goals and reality.

_____

_____

_____

_____

_____

_____

_____

_____

_____

_____

_____

_____

_____

_____

_____

_____

_____

_____

_____

_____

_____

_____

# Being a Role Model

The more we help others feel good, the better we feel, and the more we have to like about ourself.

Add the name of those you help or compliment to the pieces in the heart until it's full. Keep doing it and you'll never be sad or lonely for too long. Helping people stops us getting too down and sad.

How does it FEEL to see all the names of the people you've helped, just by being YOU?!

# SECTION 2: REGULAR DIARY CHECK IN PAGES

# CHECK IN

Day: _____ Mth: _____ Yr: _____

**HOW I MADE A DIFFERENCE TO SOMEONE:**

_____

_____

**WHO I EMPOWERED:**

_____

_____

**HOW I PUT MYSELF FIRST:**

_____

_____

**THE AFFIRMATION I CHOSE:**

_____

_____

**WHAT I LEARNT:**

_____

_____

**WHAT I'M GRATEFUL FOR:**

_____

_____

**THOUGHTS & REFLECTIONS:**

_____

_____

_____

_____

_____

_____

_____

_____

_____

_____

_____

_____

_____

_____

_____

_____

_____

_____

*You're literally a miracle of nature! Remember that!*

# CHECK IN

Day: _____ Mth: _____ Yr: _____

**HOW I MADE A DIFFERENCE TO SOMEONE:**
_____
_____

**WHO I EMPOWERED:**                    **HOW I PUT MYSELF FIRST:**
_____            _____
_____            _____

**THE AFFIRMATION I CHOSE:**
_____
_____

**WHAT I LEARNT:**                      **WHAT I'M GRATEFUL FOR:**
_____            _____
_____            _____

**THOUGHTS & REFLECTIONS:**
_____
_____
_____
_____
_____
_____
_____
_____
_____
_____
_____
_____
_____
_____
_____
_____
_____
_____

# CHECK IN

Day: _____ Mth: _____ Yr: _____

**HOW I MADE A DIFFERENCE TO SOMEONE:**
_____
_____

**WHO I EMPOWERED:**                **HOW I PUT MYSELF FIRST:**
_____           _____
_____           _____

**THE AFFIRMATION I CHOSE:**
_____
_____

**WHAT I LEARNT:**                  **WHAT I'M GRATEFUL FOR:**
_____           _____
_____           _____

**THOUGHTS & REFLECTIONS:**
_____
_____
_____
_____
_____
_____
_____
_____
_____
_____
_____
_____
_____
_____
_____
_____
_____
_____

# CHECK IN

Day: _____ Mth: _____ Yr: _____

**HOW I MADE A DIFFERENCE TO SOMEONE:**
_____
_____

**WHO I EMPOWERED:**                    **HOW I PUT MYSELF FIRST:**
_____          _____
_____          _____

**THE AFFIRMATION I CHOSE:**
_____
_____

**WHAT I LEARNT:**                      **WHAT I'M GRATEFUL FOR:**
_____          _____
_____          _____

**THOUGHTS & REFLECTIONS:**
_____
_____
_____
_____
_____
_____
_____
_____
_____
_____
_____
_____
_____
_____
_____
_____
_____
_____

# CHECK IN

Day: ———— Mth: ———— Yr: ————

**HOW I MADE A DIFFERENCE TO SOMEONE:**

_____

_____

**WHO I EMPOWERED:**

_____

_____

**HOW I PUT MYSELF FIRST:**

_____

_____

**THE AFFIRMATION I CHOSE:**

_____

_____

**WHAT I LEARNT:**

_____

_____

**WHAT I'M GRATEFUL FOR:**

_____

_____

**THOUGHTS & REFLECTIONS:**

_____

_____

_____

_____

_____

_____

_____

_____

_____

_____

_____

_____

_____

_____

_____

_____

_____

# CHECK IN

Day: _____ Mth: _____ Yr: _____

**HOW I MADE A DIFFERENCE TO SOMEONE:**

_____

_____

**WHO I EMPOWERED:**                    **HOW I PUT MYSELF FIRST:**

_____        _____

_____        _____

**THE AFFIRMATION I CHOSE:**

_____

_____

**WHAT I LEARNT:**                      **WHAT I'M GRATEFUL FOR:**

_____        _____

_____        _____

**THOUGHTS & REFLECTIONS:**

_____

_____

_____

_____

_____

_____

_____

_____

_____

_____

_____

_____

_____

_____

_____

_____

_____

26

# CHECK IN

Day: _____ Mth: _____ Yr: _____

**HOW I MADE A DIFFERENCE TO SOMEONE:**

_____

_____

**WHO I EMPOWERED:**

_____

_____

**HOW I PUT MYSELF FIRST:**

_____

_____

**THE AFFIRMATION I CHOSE:**

_____

_____

**WHAT I LEARNT:**

_____

_____

**WHAT I'M GRATEFUL FOR:**

_____

_____

**THOUGHTS & REFLECTIONS:**

_____

_____

_____

_____

_____

_____

_____

_____

_____

_____

_____

_____

_____

_____

_____

_____

_____

# CHECK IN

Day: _____ Mth: _____ Yr: _____

**HOW I MADE A DIFFERENCE TO SOMEONE:**

_____

_____

**WHO I EMPOWERED:**

_____

_____

**HOW I PUT MYSELF FIRST:**

_____

_____

**THE AFFIRMATION I CHOSE:**

_____

_____

**WHAT I LEARNT:**

_____

_____

**WHAT I'M GRATEFUL FOR:**

_____

_____

**THOUGHTS & REFLECTIONS:**

_____

_____

_____

_____

_____

_____

_____

_____

_____

_____

_____

_____

_____

_____

_____

_____

_____

# CHECK IN

Day: _____ Mth: _____ Yr: _____

**HOW I MADE A DIFFERENCE TO SOMEONE:**

_____

_____

**WHO I EMPOWERED:**

_____

_____

**HOW I PUT MYSELF FIRST:**

_____

_____

**THE AFFIRMATION I CHOSE:**

_____

_____

**WHAT I LEARNT:**

_____

_____

**WHAT I'M GRATEFUL FOR:**

_____

_____

**THOUGHTS & REFLECTIONS:**

_____

_____

_____

_____

_____

_____

_____

_____

_____

_____

_____

_____

_____

_____

_____

_____

_____

# CHECK IN

Day: _____ Mth: _____ Yr: _____

**HOW I MADE A DIFFERENCE TO SOMEONE:**

_____

_____

**WHO I EMPOWERED:**                    **HOW I PUT MYSELF FIRST:**

_____    _____

_____    _____

**THE AFFIRMATION I CHOSE:**

_____

_____

**WHAT I LEARNT:**                    **WHAT I'M GRATEFUL FOR:**

_____    _____

_____    _____

**THOUGHTS & REFLECTIONS:**

_____

_____

_____

_____

_____

_____

_____

_____

_____

_____

_____

_____

_____

_____

_____

_____

_____

_____

# CHECK IN

Day: _____ Mth: _____ Yr: _____

**HOW I MADE A DIFFERENCE TO SOMEONE:**

_____

_____

**WHO I EMPOWERED:**

_____

_____

**HOW I PUT MYSELF FIRST:**

_____

_____

**THE AFFIRMATION I CHOSE:**

_____

_____

**WHAT I LEARNT:**

_____

_____

**WHAT I'M GRATEFUL FOR:**

_____

_____

**THOUGHTS & REFLECTIONS:**

_____

_____

_____

_____

_____

_____

_____

_____

_____

_____

_____

_____

_____

_____

_____

_____

_____

*Love yourself how you want to be loved!*

# CHECK IN

Day: _____ Mth: _____ Yr: _____

**HOW I MADE A DIFFERENCE TO SOMEONE:**

_____

_____

**WHO I EMPOWERED:**

_____

_____

**HOW I PUT MYSELF FIRST:**

_____

_____

**THE AFFIRMATION I CHOSE:**

_____

_____

**WHAT I LEARNT:**

_____

_____

**WHAT I'M GRATEFUL FOR:**

_____

_____

**THOUGHTS & REFLECTIONS:**

_____

_____

_____

_____

_____

_____

_____

_____

_____

_____

_____

_____

_____

_____

_____

_____

# CHECK IN

Day: _____ Mth: _____ Yr: _____

**HOW I MADE A DIFFERENCE TO SOMEONE:**

_____

_____

**WHO I EMPOWERED:**

_____

_____

**HOW I PUT MYSELF FIRST:**

_____

_____

**THE AFFIRMATION I CHOSE:**

_____

_____

**WHAT I LEARNT:**

_____

_____

**WHAT I'M GRATEFUL FOR:**

_____

_____

**THOUGHTS & REFLECTIONS:**

_____

_____

_____

_____

_____

_____

_____

_____

_____

_____

_____

_____

_____

_____

_____

_____

_____

_____

_____

# CHECK IN

Day: _____ Mth: _____ Yr: _____

**HOW I MADE A DIFFERENCE TO SOMEONE:**

_____

_____

**WHO I EMPOWERED:**

_____

**HOW I PUT MYSELF FIRST:**

_____

**THE AFFIRMATION I CHOSE:**

_____

**WHAT I LEARNT:**

_____

**WHAT I'M GRATEFUL FOR:**

_____

**THOUGHTS & REFLECTIONS:**

_____

_____

_____

_____

_____

_____

_____

_____

_____

_____

_____

_____

_____

_____

_____

# CHECK IN

Day: _____ Mth: _____ Yr: _____

**HOW I MADE A DIFFERENCE TO SOMEONE:**

_____

_____

**WHO I EMPOWERED:**          **HOW I PUT MYSELF FIRST:**

_____    _____

_____    _____

**THE AFFIRMATION I CHOSE:**

_____

_____

**WHAT I LEARNT:**          **WHAT I'M GRATEFUL FOR:**

_____    _____

_____    _____

**THOUGHTS & REFLECTIONS:**

_____

_____

_____

_____

_____

_____

_____

_____

_____

_____

_____

_____

_____

_____

_____

_____

_____

_____

# CHECK IN

Day: _____ Mth: _____ Yr: _____

**HOW I MADE A DIFFERENCE TO SOMEONE:**

_____

_____

**WHO I EMPOWERED:**

**HOW I PUT MYSELF FIRST:**

_____

_____

_____

_____

**THE AFFIRMATION I CHOSE:**

_____

_____

**WHAT I LEARNT:**

**WHAT I'M GRATEFUL FOR:**

_____

_____

_____

_____

**THOUGHTS & REFLECTIONS:**

_____

_____

_____

_____

_____

_____

_____

_____

_____

_____

_____

_____

_____

_____

_____

_____

_____

# CHECK IN

Day: _____ Mth: _____ Yr: _____

**HOW I MADE A DIFFERENCE TO SOMEONE:**

_____

_____

**WHO I EMPOWERED:**

_____

_____

**HOW I PUT MYSELF FIRST:**

_____

_____

**THE AFFIRMATION I CHOSE:**

_____

_____

**WHAT I LEARNT:**

_____

_____

**WHAT I'M GRATEFUL FOR:**

_____

_____

**THOUGHTS & REFLECTIONS:**

_____

_____

_____

_____

_____

_____

_____

_____

_____

_____

_____

_____

_____

_____

_____

_____

_____

# CHECK IN

Day: _____ Mth: _____ Yr: _____

**HOW I MADE A DIFFERENCE TO SOMEONE:**

_____

_____

**WHO I EMPOWERED:**                **HOW I PUT MYSELF FIRST:**

_____            _____

_____            _____

**THE AFFIRMATION I CHOSE:**

_____

_____

**WHAT I LEARNT:**                  **WHAT I'M GRATEFUL FOR:**

_____            _____

_____            _____

**THOUGHTS & REFLECTIONS:**

_____

_____

_____

_____

_____

_____

_____

_____

_____

_____

_____

_____

_____

_____

_____

_____

# CHECK IN

Day: _____ Mth: _____ Yr: _____

**HOW I MADE A DIFFERENCE TO SOMEONE:**
_____
_____

**WHO I EMPOWERED:**                    **HOW I PUT MYSELF FIRST:**
_____                _____
_____                _____

**THE AFFIRMATION I CHOSE:**
_____
_____

**WHAT I LEARNT:**                       **WHAT I'M GRATEFUL FOR:**
_____                _____
_____                _____

**THOUGHTS & REFLECTIONS:**
_____
_____
_____
_____
_____
_____
_____
_____
_____
_____
_____
_____
_____
_____
_____
_____
_____
_____

# CHECK IN

Day: _____ Mth: _____ Yr: _____

**HOW I MADE A DIFFERENCE TO SOMEONE:**

_____

_____

**WHO I EMPOWERED:**

_____

_____

**HOW I PUT MYSELF FIRST:**

_____

_____

**THE AFFIRMATION I CHOSE:**

_____

_____

**WHAT I LEARNT:**

_____

_____

**WHAT I'M GRATEFUL FOR:**

_____

_____

**THOUGHTS & REFLECTIONS:**

_____

_____

_____

_____

_____

_____

_____

_____

_____

_____

_____

_____

_____

_____

_____

# CHECK IN

Day: _____ Mth: _____ Yr: _____

**HOW I MADE A DIFFERENCE TO SOMEONE:**

_____

_____

**WHO I EMPOWERED:**

_____

_____

**HOW I PUT MYSELF FIRST:**

_____

_____

**THE AFFIRMATION I CHOSE:**

_____

_____

**WHAT I LEARNT:**

_____

_____

**WHAT I'M GRATEFUL FOR:**

_____

_____

**THOUGHTS & REFLECTIONS:**

_____

_____

_____

_____

_____

_____

_____

_____

_____

_____

_____

_____

_____

_____

_____

_____

_____

*You're the ocean, not the ship*

# CHECK IN

Day: _____ Mth: _____ Yr: _____

**HOW I MADE A DIFFERENCE TO SOMEONE:**

_____

_____

**WHO I EMPOWERED:**

_____

_____

**HOW I PUT MYSELF FIRST:**

_____

_____

**THE AFFIRMATION I CHOSE:**

_____

_____

**WHAT I LEARNT:**

_____

_____

**WHAT I'M GRATEFUL FOR:**

_____

_____

**THOUGHTS & REFLECTIONS:**

_____

_____

_____

_____

_____

_____

_____

_____

_____

_____

_____

_____

_____

_____

_____

_____

_____

# CHECK IN

Day: _____ Mth: _____ Yr: _____

**HOW I MADE A DIFFERENCE TO SOMEONE:**

_____

_____

**WHO I EMPOWERED:**

_____

_____

**HOW I PUT MYSELF FIRST:**

_____

_____

**THE AFFIRMATION I CHOSE:**

_____

_____

**WHAT I LEARNT:**

_____

_____

**WHAT I'M GRATEFUL FOR:**

_____

_____

**THOUGHTS & REFLECTIONS:**

_____

_____

_____

_____

_____

_____

_____

_____

_____

_____

_____

_____

_____

_____

_____

_____

# CHECK IN

Day: _____ Mth: _____ Yr: _____

**HOW I MADE A DIFFERENCE TO SOMEONE:**

_____

_____

**WHO I EMPOWERED:**

_____

_____

**HOW I PUT MYSELF FIRST:**

_____

_____

**THE AFFIRMATION I CHOSE:**

_____

_____

**WHAT I LEARNT:**

_____

_____

**WHAT I'M GRATEFUL FOR:**

_____

_____

**THOUGHTS & REFLECTIONS:**

_____

_____

_____

_____

_____

_____

_____

_____

_____

_____

_____

_____

_____

_____

_____

_____

_____

# CHECK IN

Day: _____ Mth: _____ Yr: _____

**HOW I MADE A DIFFERENCE TO SOMEONE:**

_____

_____

**WHO I EMPOWERED:**

_____

_____

**HOW I PUT MYSELF FIRST:**

_____

_____

**THE AFFIRMATION I CHOSE:**

_____

_____

**WHAT I LEARNT:**

_____

_____

**WHAT I'M GRATEFUL FOR:**

_____

_____

**THOUGHTS & REFLECTIONS:**

_____

_____

_____

_____

_____

_____

_____

_____

_____

_____

_____

_____

_____

_____

_____

_____

_____

# CHECK IN

Day: _____ Mth: _____ Yr: _____

**HOW I MADE A DIFFERENCE TO SOMEONE:**

_____

_____

**WHO I EMPOWERED:**

_____

_____

**HOW I PUT MYSELF FIRST:**

_____

_____

**THE AFFIRMATION I CHOSE:**

_____

_____

**WHAT I LEARNT:**

_____

_____

**WHAT I'M GRATEFUL FOR:**

_____

_____

**THOUGHTS & REFLECTIONS:**

_____

_____

_____

_____

_____

_____

_____

_____

_____

_____

_____

_____

_____

_____

_____

_____

_____

# CHECK IN

Day: _____ Mth: _____ Yr: _____

**HOW I MADE A DIFFERENCE TO SOMEONE:**

_____

_____

**WHO I EMPOWERED:**

_____

_____

**HOW I PUT MYSELF FIRST:**

_____

_____

**THE AFFIRMATION I CHOSE:**

_____

_____

**WHAT I LEARNT:**

_____

_____

**WHAT I'M GRATEFUL FOR:**

_____

_____

**THOUGHTS & REFLECTIONS:**

_____

_____

_____

_____

_____

_____

_____

_____

_____

_____

_____

_____

_____

_____

_____

_____

# CHECK IN

Day: _____ Mth: _____ Yr: _____

**HOW I MADE A DIFFERENCE TO SOMEONE:**
_____
_____

**WHO I EMPOWERED:**
_____

**HOW I PUT MYSELF FIRST:**
_____

**THE AFFIRMATION I CHOSE:**
_____
_____

**WHAT I LEARNT:**
_____

**WHAT I'M GRATEFUL FOR:**
_____

**THOUGHTS & REFLECTIONS:**
_____
_____
_____
_____
_____
_____
_____
_____
_____
_____
_____
_____
_____
_____
_____
_____

# CHECK IN

Day: _____ Mth: _____ Yr: _____

**HOW I MADE A DIFFERENCE TO SOMEONE:**

_____

_____

**WHO I EMPOWERED:**                    **HOW I PUT MYSELF FIRST:**

_____              _____

_____              _____

**THE AFFIRMATION I CHOSE:**

_____

_____

**WHAT I LEARNT:**                      **WHAT I'M GRATEFUL FOR:**

_____              _____

_____              _____

**THOUGHTS & REFLECTIONS:**

_____

_____

_____

_____

_____

_____

_____

_____

_____

_____

_____

_____

_____

_____

_____

_____

# CHECK IN

Day: _____ Mth: _____ Yr: _____

**HOW I MADE A DIFFERENCE TO SOMEONE:**

_____

_____

**WHO I EMPOWERED:**

_____

_____

**HOW I PUT MYSELF FIRST:**

_____

_____

**THE AFFIRMATION I CHOSE:**

_____

**WHAT I LEARNT:**

_____

_____

**WHAT I'M GRATEFUL FOR:**

_____

_____

**THOUGHTS & REFLECTIONS:**

_____

_____

_____

_____

_____

_____

_____

_____

_____

_____

_____

_____

_____

_____

_____

_____

# CHECK IN

Day: _____ Mth: _____ Yr: _____

**HOW I MADE A DIFFERENCE TO SOMEONE:**
_____
_____

**WHO I EMPOWERED:**                    **HOW I PUT MYSELF FIRST:**
_____        _____
_____        _____

**THE AFFIRMATION I CHOSE:**
_____
_____

**WHAT I LEARNT:**                      **WHAT I'M GRATEFUL FOR:**
_____        _____
_____        _____

**THOUGHTS & REFLECTIONS:**
_____
_____
_____
_____
_____
_____
_____
_____
_____
_____
_____
_____
_____
_____
_____
_____
_____
_____

*You're literally one in more than a billion!*

# CHECK IN

Day: _____ Mth: _____ Yr: _____

**HOW I MADE A DIFFERENCE TO SOMEONE:**

_____

_____

**WHO I EMPOWERED:**

_____

_____

**HOW I PUT MYSELF FIRST:**

_____

_____

**THE AFFIRMATION I CHOSE:**

_____

_____

**WHAT I LEARNT:**

_____

_____

**WHAT I'M GRATEFUL FOR:**

_____

_____

**THOUGHTS & REFLECTIONS:**

_____

_____

_____

_____

_____

_____

_____

_____

_____

_____

_____

_____

_____

_____

_____

_____

_____

# CHECK IN

Day: _____ Mth: _____ Yr: _____

**HOW I MADE A DIFFERENCE TO SOMEONE:**

_____

_____

**WHO I EMPOWERED:**                    **HOW I PUT MYSELF FIRST:**

_____          _____

_____          _____

**THE AFFIRMATION I CHOSE:**

_____

_____

**WHAT I LEARNT:**                      **WHAT I'M GRATEFUL FOR:**

_____          _____

_____          _____

**THOUGHTS & REFLECTIONS:**

_____

_____

_____

_____

_____

_____

_____

_____

_____

_____

_____

_____

_____

_____

_____

_____

_____

# CHECK IN

Day: _____ Mth: _____ Yr: _____

**HOW I MADE A DIFFERENCE TO SOMEONE:**

_____

_____

**WHO I EMPOWERED:**                    **HOW I PUT MYSELF FIRST:**

_____            _____

_____            _____

**THE AFFIRMATION I CHOSE:**

_____

_____

**WHAT I LEARNT:**                      **WHAT I'M GRATEFUL FOR:**

_____            _____

_____            _____

**THOUGHTS & REFLECTIONS:**

_____

_____

_____

_____

_____

_____

_____

_____

_____

_____

_____

_____

_____

_____

_____

_____

# CHECK IN

Day: _____ Mth: _____ Yr: _____

**HOW I MADE A DIFFERENCE TO SOMEONE:**

_____

_____

**WHO I EMPOWERED:**

**HOW I PUT MYSELF FIRST:**

**THE AFFIRMATION I CHOSE:**

**WHAT I LEARNT:**

**WHAT I'M GRATEFUL FOR:**

**THOUGHTS & REFLECTIONS:**

# CHECK IN

Day: _____ Mth: _____ Yr: _____

**HOW I MADE A DIFFERENCE TO SOMEONE:**

_____

_____

**WHO I EMPOWERED:**

**HOW I PUT MYSELF FIRST:**

_____     _____

_____     _____

**THE AFFIRMATION I CHOSE:**

_____

_____

**WHAT I LEARNT:**

**WHAT I'M GRATEFUL FOR:**

_____     _____

_____     _____

**THOUGHTS & REFLECTIONS:**

_____

_____

_____

_____

_____

_____

_____

_____

_____

_____

_____

_____

_____

_____

_____

_____

_____

_____

# CHECK IN

Day: _____  Mth: _____  Yr: _____

**HOW I MADE A DIFFERENCE TO SOMEONE:**
_____
_____

**WHO I EMPOWERED:**                    **HOW I PUT MYSELF FIRST:**
_____                _____
_____                _____

**THE AFFIRMATION I CHOSE:**
_____
_____

**WHAT I LEARNT:**                       **WHAT I'M GRATEFUL FOR:**
_____                _____
_____                _____

**THOUGHTS & REFLECTIONS:**
_____
_____
_____
_____
_____
_____
_____
_____
_____
_____
_____
_____
_____
_____
_____
_____
_____

# CHECK IN

Day: _____ Mth: _____ Yr: _____

**HOW I MADE A DIFFERENCE TO SOMEONE:**

_____

_____

**WHO I EMPOWERED:**                    **HOW I PUT MYSELF FIRST:**

_____            _____

_____            _____

**THE AFFIRMATION I CHOSE:**

_____

_____

**WHAT I LEARNT:**                      **WHAT I'M GRATEFUL FOR:**

_____            _____

_____            _____

**THOUGHTS & REFLECTIONS:**

_____

_____

_____

_____

_____

_____

_____

_____

_____

_____

_____

_____

_____

_____

_____

_____

_____

# CHECK IN

Day: _____ Mth: _____ Yr: _____

**HOW I MADE A DIFFERENCE TO SOMEONE:**

_____

_____

**WHO I EMPOWERED:**

_____

_____

**THE AFFIRMATION I CHOSE:**

_____

_____

**WHAT I LEARNT:**

_____

_____

**HOW I PUT MYSELF FIRST:**

_____

_____

**WHAT I'M GRATEFUL FOR:**

_____

_____

**THOUGHTS & REFLECTIONS:**

_____

_____

_____

_____

_____

_____

_____

_____

_____

_____

_____

_____

_____

_____

_____

_____

# CHECK IN

Day: _____ Mth: _____ Yr: _____

**HOW I MADE A DIFFERENCE TO SOMEONE:**

_____

_____

**WHO I EMPOWERED:**                **HOW I PUT MYSELF FIRST:**

_____            _____

_____            _____

**THE AFFIRMATION I CHOSE:**

_____

_____

**WHAT I LEARNT:**                  **WHAT I'M GRATEFUL FOR:**

_____            _____

_____            _____

**THOUGHTS & REFLECTIONS:**

_____

_____

_____

_____

_____

_____

_____

_____

_____

_____

_____

_____

_____

_____

_____

_____

_____

# CHECK IN

Day: _____ Mth: _____ Yr: _____

**HOW I MADE A DIFFERENCE TO SOMEONE:**

_____

_____

**WHO I EMPOWERED:**

_____

_____

**HOW I PUT MYSELF FIRST:**

_____

_____

**THE AFFIRMATION I CHOSE:**

_____

_____

**WHAT I LEARNT:**

_____

_____

**WHAT I'M GRATEFUL FOR:**

_____

_____

**THOUGHTS & REFLECTIONS:**

_____

_____

_____

_____

_____

_____

_____

_____

_____

_____

_____

_____

_____

_____

_____

_____

_____

_____

*The little girl you were, didn't die; she's in those pupil pits in the mirror. Adopt her and love her like she still deserves to be.*

# CHECK IN

Day: _____ Mth: _____ Yr: _____

**HOW I MADE A DIFFERENCE TO SOMEONE:**

_____

_____

**WHO I EMPOWERED:**

_____

_____

**HOW I PUT MYSELF FIRST:**

_____

_____

**THE AFFIRMATION I CHOSE:**

_____

_____

**WHAT I LEARNT:**

_____

_____

**WHAT I'M GRATEFUL FOR:**

_____

_____

**THOUGHTS & REFLECTIONS:**

_____

_____

_____

_____

_____

_____

_____

_____

_____

_____

_____

_____

_____

_____

_____

_____

_____

_____

# CHECK IN

Day: _____ Mth: _____ Yr: _____

**HOW I MADE A DIFFERENCE TO SOMEONE:**

_____

_____

**WHO I EMPOWERED:**

_____

_____

**HOW I PUT MYSELF FIRST:**

_____

_____

**THE AFFIRMATION I CHOSE:**

_____

_____

**WHAT I LEARNT:**

_____

_____

**WHAT I'M GRATEFUL FOR:**

_____

_____

**THOUGHTS & REFLECTIONS:**

_____

_____

_____

_____

_____

_____

_____

_____

_____

_____

_____

_____

_____

_____

_____

_____

_____

# CHECK IN

Day: _____ Mth: _____ Yr: _____

**HOW I MADE A DIFFERENCE TO SOMEONE:**

_____

_____

**WHO I EMPOWERED:**

**HOW I PUT MYSELF FIRST:**

_____

_____

**THE AFFIRMATION I CHOSE:**

_____

_____

**WHAT I LEARNT:**

**WHAT I'M GRATEFUL FOR:**

_____

_____

**THOUGHTS & REFLECTIONS:**

_____

_____

_____

_____

_____

_____

_____

_____

_____

_____

_____

_____

_____

_____

_____

_____

# CHECK IN

Day: _____ Mth: _____ Yr: _____

**HOW I MADE A DIFFERENCE TO SOMEONE:**

_____

_____

**WHO I EMPOWERED:**

_____

_____

**HOW I PUT MYSELF FIRST:**

_____

_____

**THE AFFIRMATION I CHOSE:**

_____

_____

**WHAT I LEARNT:**

_____

_____

**WHAT I'M GRATEFUL FOR:**

_____

_____

**THOUGHTS & REFLECTIONS:**

_____

_____

_____

_____

_____

_____

_____

_____

_____

_____

_____

_____

_____

_____

_____

# CHECK IN

Day: _____ Mth: _____ Yr: _____

**HOW I MADE A DIFFERENCE TO SOMEONE:**

_____

_____

**WHO I EMPOWERED:**                    **HOW I PUT MYSELF FIRST:**

_____              _____

_____              _____

**THE AFFIRMATION I CHOSE:**

_____

_____

**WHAT I LEARNT:**                      **WHAT I'M GRATEFUL FOR:**

_____              _____

_____              _____

**THOUGHTS & REFLECTIONS:**

_____

_____

_____

_____

_____

_____

_____

_____

_____

_____

_____

_____

_____

_____

_____

_____

_____

# CHECK IN

Day: _____ Mth: _____ Yr: _____

**HOW I MADE A DIFFERENCE TO SOMEONE:**

_____

_____

**WHO I EMPOWERED:**

_____

_____

**HOW I PUT MYSELF FIRST:**

_____

_____

**THE AFFIRMATION I CHOSE:**

_____

_____

**WHAT I LEARNT:**

_____

_____

**WHAT I'M GRATEFUL FOR:**

_____

_____

**THOUGHTS & REFLECTIONS:**

_____

_____

_____

_____

_____

_____

_____

_____

_____

_____

_____

_____

_____

_____

_____

_____

# CHECK IN

Day: _____ Mth: _____ Yr: _____

**HOW I MADE A DIFFERENCE TO SOMEONE:**

_____

_____

**WHO I EMPOWERED:**                    **HOW I PUT MYSELF FIRST:**

_____          _____

_____          _____

**THE AFFIRMATION I CHOSE:**

_____

_____

**WHAT I LEARNT:**                      **WHAT I'M GRATEFUL FOR:**

_____          _____

_____          _____

**THOUGHTS & REFLECTIONS:**

_____

_____

_____

_____

_____

_____

_____

_____

_____

_____

_____

_____

_____

_____

_____

_____

_____

# CHECK IN

Day: _____ Mth: _____ Yr: _____

**HOW I MADE A DIFFERENCE TO SOMEONE:**

_____

_____

**WHO I EMPOWERED:**

_____

_____

**HOW I PUT MYSELF FIRST:**

_____

_____

**THE AFFIRMATION I CHOSE:**

_____

_____

**WHAT I LEARNT:**

_____

_____

**WHAT I'M GRATEFUL FOR:**

_____

_____

**THOUGHTS & REFLECTIONS:**

_____

_____

_____

_____

_____

_____

_____

_____

_____

_____

_____

_____

_____

_____

_____

_____

_____

_____

# CHECK IN

Day: _____ Mth: _____ Yr: _____

**HOW I MADE A DIFFERENCE TO SOMEONE:**
_____
_____

**WHO I EMPOWERED:**                    **HOW I PUT MYSELF FIRST:**
_____            _____
_____            _____

**THE AFFIRMATION I CHOSE:**
_____
_____

**WHAT I LEARNT:**                      **WHAT I'M GRATEFUL FOR:**
_____            _____
_____            _____

**THOUGHTS & REFLECTIONS:**
_____
_____
_____
_____
_____
_____
_____
_____
_____
_____
_____
_____
_____
_____
_____
_____
_____

# CHECK IN

Day: _____ Mth: _____ Yr: _____

**HOW I MADE A DIFFERENCE TO SOMEONE:**

_____

_____

**WHO I EMPOWERED:**

_____

**HOW I PUT MYSELF FIRST:**

_____

**THE AFFIRMATION I CHOSE:**

_____

_____

**WHAT I LEARNT:**

_____

**WHAT I'M GRATEFUL FOR:**

_____

**THOUGHTS & REFLECTIONS:**

_____

_____

_____

_____

_____

_____

_____

_____

_____

_____

_____

_____

_____

_____

_____

_____

_____

*Roll with it; it always works out*

# CHECK IN

Day: _____ Mth: _____ Yr: _____

**HOW I MADE A DIFFERENCE TO SOMEONE:**
_____
_____

**WHO I EMPOWERED:**                    **HOW I PUT MYSELF FIRST:**
_____           _____
_____           _____

**THE AFFIRMATION I CHOSE:**
_____
_____

**WHAT I LEARNT:**                      **WHAT I'M GRATEFUL FOR:**
_____           _____
_____           _____

**THOUGHTS & REFLECTIONS:**
_____
_____
_____
_____
_____
_____
_____
_____
_____
_____
_____
_____
_____
_____
_____
_____
_____
_____

# CHECK IN

Day: _____ Mth: _____ Yr: _____

**HOW I MADE A DIFFERENCE TO SOMEONE:**

_____

_____

**WHO I EMPOWERED:**

_____

_____

**HOW I PUT MYSELF FIRST:**

_____

_____

**THE AFFIRMATION I CHOSE:**

_____

_____

**WHAT I LEARNT:**

_____

_____

**WHAT I'M GRATEFUL FOR:**

_____

_____

**THOUGHTS & REFLECTIONS:**

_____

_____

_____

_____

_____

_____

_____

_____

_____

_____

_____

_____

_____

_____

_____

_____

_____

_____

# CHECK IN

Day: _____ Mth: _____ Yr: _____

**HOW I MADE A DIFFERENCE TO SOMEONE:**

_____

_____

**WHO I EMPOWERED:**

_____

_____

**HOW I PUT MYSELF FIRST:**

_____

_____

**THE AFFIRMATION I CHOSE:**

_____

_____

**WHAT I LEARNT:**

_____

_____

**WHAT I'M GRATEFUL FOR:**

_____

_____

**THOUGHTS & REFLECTIONS:**

_____

_____

_____

_____

_____

_____

_____

_____

_____

_____

_____

_____

_____

_____

_____

_____

_____

_____

# CHECK IN

Day: _____  Mth: _____  Yr: _____

**HOW I MADE A DIFFERENCE TO SOMEONE:**
_____
_____

**WHO I EMPOWERED:**                    **HOW I PUT MYSELF FIRST:**
_____               _____
_____               _____

**THE AFFIRMATION I CHOSE:**
_____
_____

**WHAT I LEARNT:**                      **WHAT I'M GRATEFUL FOR:**
_____               _____
_____               _____

**THOUGHTS & REFLECTIONS:**
_____
_____
_____
_____
_____
_____
_____
_____
_____
_____
_____
_____
_____
_____
_____
_____
_____
_____

# CHECK IN

Day: _____ Mth: _____ Yr: _____

**HOW I MADE A DIFFERENCE TO SOMEONE:**

_____

_____

**WHO I EMPOWERED:**

_____

_____

**HOW I PUT MYSELF FIRST:**

_____

_____

**THE AFFIRMATION I CHOSE:**

_____

_____

**WHAT I LEARNT:**

_____

_____

**WHAT I'M GRATEFUL FOR:**

_____

_____

**THOUGHTS & REFLECTIONS:**

_____

_____

_____

_____

_____

_____

_____

_____

_____

_____

_____

_____

_____

_____

_____

_____

_____

# CHECK IN

Day: _____ Mth: _____ Yr: _____

**HOW I MADE A DIFFERENCE TO SOMEONE:**

_____

_____

**WHO I EMPOWERED:**

_____

_____

**HOW I PUT MYSELF FIRST:**

_____

_____

**THE AFFIRMATION I CHOSE:**

_____

_____

**WHAT I LEARNT:**

_____

_____

**WHAT I'M GRATEFUL FOR:**

_____

_____

**THOUGHTS & REFLECTIONS:**

_____

_____

_____

_____

_____

_____

_____

_____

_____

_____

_____

_____

_____

_____

_____

_____

_____

_____

# CHECK IN

Day: _____ Mth: _____ Yr: _____

**HOW I MADE A DIFFERENCE TO SOMEONE:**

_____

_____

**WHO I EMPOWERED:**

_____

_____

**HOW I PUT MYSELF FIRST:**

_____

_____

**THE AFFIRMATION I CHOSE:**

_____

_____

**WHAT I LEARNT:**

_____

_____

**WHAT I'M GRATEFUL FOR:**

_____

_____

**THOUGHTS & REFLECTIONS:**

_____

_____

_____

_____

_____

_____

_____

_____

_____

_____

_____

_____

_____

_____

_____

_____

_____

# CHECK IN

Day: _____ Mth: _____ Yr: _____

**HOW I MADE A DIFFERENCE TO SOMEONE:**

_____

_____

**WHO I EMPOWERED:**

_____

_____

**HOW I PUT MYSELF FIRST:**

_____

_____

**THE AFFIRMATION I CHOSE:**

_____

_____

**WHAT I LEARNT:**

_____

_____

**WHAT I'M GRATEFUL FOR:**

_____

_____

**THOUGHTS & REFLECTIONS:**

_____

_____

_____

_____

_____

_____

_____

_____

_____

_____

_____

_____

_____

_____

_____

_____

_____

_____

# CHECK IN

Day: _____ Mth: _____ Yr: _____

**HOW I MADE A DIFFERENCE TO SOMEONE:**

_____

_____

**WHO I EMPOWERED:**                    **HOW I PUT MYSELF FIRST:**

_____        _____

_____        _____

**THE AFFIRMATION I CHOSE:**

_____

_____

**WHAT I LEARNT:**                      **WHAT I'M GRATEFUL FOR:**

_____        _____

_____        _____

**THOUGHTS & REFLECTIONS:**

_____

_____

_____

_____

_____

_____

_____

_____

_____

_____

_____

_____

_____

_____

_____

_____

# CHECK IN

Day: _____ Mth: _____ Yr: _____

**HOW I MADE A DIFFERENCE TO SOMEONE:**

_____

_____

**WHO I EMPOWERED:**

_____

_____

**HOW I PUT MYSELF FIRST:**

_____

_____

**THE AFFIRMATION I CHOSE:**

_____

**WHAT I LEARNT:**

_____

_____

**WHAT I'M GRATEFUL FOR:**

_____

_____

**THOUGHTS & REFLECTIONS:**

_____

_____

_____

_____

_____

_____

_____

_____

_____

_____

_____

_____

_____

_____

_____

*Be your own best friend*

# CHECK IN

Day: _____ Mth: _____ Yr: _____

**HOW I MADE A DIFFERENCE TO SOMEONE:**

_____
_____

**WHO I EMPOWERED:**

_____

_____

**HOW I PUT MYSELF FIRST:**

_____

_____

**THE AFFIRMATION I CHOSE:**

_____
_____

**WHAT I LEARNT:**

_____

_____

**WHAT I'M GRATEFUL FOR:**

_____

_____

**THOUGHTS & REFLECTIONS:**

_____
_____
_____
_____
_____
_____
_____
_____
_____
_____
_____
_____
_____
_____
_____
_____
_____

# CHECK IN

Day: _____ Mth: _____ Yr: _____

**HOW I MADE A DIFFERENCE TO SOMEONE:**

_____

_____

**WHO I EMPOWERED:**                          **HOW I PUT MYSELF FIRST:**

_____          _____

_____          _____

**THE AFFIRMATION I CHOSE:**

_____

_____

**WHAT I LEARNT:**                          **WHAT I'M GRATEFUL FOR:**

_____          _____

_____          _____

**THOUGHTS & REFLECTIONS:**

_____

_____

_____

_____

_____

_____

_____

_____

_____

_____

_____

_____

_____

_____

_____

_____

# CHECK IN

Day: _____ Mth: _____ Yr: _____

**HOW I MADE A DIFFERENCE TO SOMEONE:**

_____

_____

**WHO I EMPOWERED:**

_____

_____

**THE AFFIRMATION I CHOSE:**

_____

_____

**WHAT I LEARNT:**

_____

_____

**HOW I PUT MYSELF FIRST:**

_____

_____

**WHAT I'M GRATEFUL FOR:**

_____

_____

**THOUGHTS & REFLECTIONS:**

_____

_____

_____

_____

_____

_____

_____

_____

_____

_____

_____

_____

_____

_____

_____

_____

_____

# CHECK IN

Day: _____ Mth: _____ Yr: _____

**HOW I MADE A DIFFERENCE TO SOMEONE:**

_____

_____

**WHO I EMPOWERED:**

_____

_____

**HOW I PUT MYSELF FIRST:**

_____

_____

**THE AFFIRMATION I CHOSE:**

_____

_____

**WHAT I LEARNT:**

_____

_____

**WHAT I'M GRATEFUL FOR:**

_____

_____

**THOUGHTS & REFLECTIONS:**

_____

_____

_____

_____

_____

_____

_____

_____

_____

_____

_____

_____

_____

_____

_____

_____

_____

# CHECK IN

Day: _____  Mth: _____  Yr: _____

**HOW I MADE A DIFFERENCE TO SOMEONE:**
_____
_____

**WHO I EMPOWERED:**                    **HOW I PUT MYSELF FIRST:**
_____          _____
_____          _____

**THE AFFIRMATION I CHOSE:**
_____
_____

**WHAT I LEARNT:**                      **WHAT I'M GRATEFUL FOR:**
_____          _____
_____          _____

**THOUGHTS & REFLECTIONS:**
_____
_____
_____
_____
_____
_____
_____
_____
_____
_____
_____
_____
_____
_____
_____
_____
_____
_____
_____
_____

# CHECK IN

Day: _____ Mth: _____ Yr: _____

**HOW I MADE A DIFFERENCE TO SOMEONE:**

_____

_____

**WHO I EMPOWERED:**

_____

_____

**HOW I PUT MYSELF FIRST:**

_____

_____

**THE AFFIRMATION I CHOSE:**

_____

_____

**WHAT I LEARNT:**

_____

_____

**WHAT I'M GRATEFUL FOR:**

_____

_____

**THOUGHTS & REFLECTIONS:**

_____

_____

_____

_____

_____

_____

_____

_____

_____

_____

_____

_____

_____

_____

_____

_____

_____

# CHECK IN

Day: _____ Mth: _____ Yr: _____

**HOW I MADE A DIFFERENCE TO SOMEONE:**

_____

_____

**WHO I EMPOWERED:**              **HOW I PUT MYSELF FIRST:**

_____    _____

_____    _____

**THE AFFIRMATION I CHOSE:**

_____

_____

**WHAT I LEARNT:**              **WHAT I'M GRATEFUL FOR:**

_____    _____

_____    _____

**THOUGHTS & REFLECTIONS:**

_____

_____

_____

_____

_____

_____

_____

_____

_____

_____

_____

_____

_____

_____

_____

_____

# CHECK IN

Day: _____ Mth: _____ Yr: _____

**HOW I MADE A DIFFERENCE TO SOMEONE:**

_____

_____

**WHO I EMPOWERED:**

_____

_____

**HOW I PUT MYSELF FIRST:**

_____

_____

**THE AFFIRMATION I CHOSE:**

_____

_____

**WHAT I LEARNT:**

_____

_____

**WHAT I'M GRATEFUL FOR:**

_____

_____

**THOUGHTS & REFLECTIONS:**

_____

_____

_____

_____

_____

_____

_____

_____

_____

_____

_____

_____

_____

_____

_____

_____

_____

# CHECK IN

Day: _____ Mth: _____ Yr: _____

**HOW I MADE A DIFFERENCE TO SOMEONE:**

_____

_____

**WHO I EMPOWERED:**

_____

_____

**HOW I PUT MYSELF FIRST:**

_____

_____

**THE AFFIRMATION I CHOSE:**

_____

_____

**WHAT I LEARNT:**

_____

_____

**WHAT I'M GRATEFUL FOR:**

_____

_____

**THOUGHTS & REFLECTIONS:**

_____

_____

_____

_____

_____

_____

_____

_____

_____

_____

_____

_____

_____

_____

_____

_____

_____

# SECTION 3: UNDERSTANDING YOUR HORMONAL IMPACT ON EMOTIONS

# My Cycle

Your monthly cycle is NORMAL, and affects a lot of things in your life—like how you relate to others, your work, creativity, emotions, and decision-making.

It also influences your energy levels, how you see things, and your mood.

Your cycle even impacts HOW MUCH you sleep! Some days you will need more, other days, you'll function well with less.

Depending on your cycle, even how well you learn or concentrate can be affected. Things you find hard during Winter can be much easier to understand in Summer.

It's okay to do different things at different times and not try to be the same all the time.

Remember, change is normal, and you should go with it, not against it.

Be kind to yourself and use your cycle as a tool for feeling good inside.

Make notes on each Phase Page of the traits that you notice are normal for YOU.

By learning what your cycle looks like FOR YOU, you will start to create more self-acceptance of your own natural flow.

# SPRING

From the day after your period finishes, you'll start feeling better—no more aches or emotional ups and downs. It's like a fresh start after a long winter.

You'll become more optimistic and you energy will start to focus outward.

It's a great time for personal goals, especially short-term ones. You'll find it easy to stay positive, take action, and not stress about small things.

Your physical stamina increases, making you more independent.

While you may feel less empathetic, your concentration and logical thinking improve.

You'll start to notice an improvement in what you're able to learn, and how you're able to express yourself.

Trust yourself more, and try new things.

It's natural that you'll have less need for sleep.

This is a great week to break bad habits because you'll feel strong.

# SUMMER

This week, your estrogen is at its peak. You'll feel really good—confident and energetic.

You'll see the world positively and your positive vibes will boost your projects and relationships, making people enjoy being around you.

You'll have less patience for drama, because you just want to make the most of life.

Share your dreams, plan, and write.

You'll be grateful and joyful, naturally.

Connect with your family and boost your confidence through self-reflection.

This is a great week to use your Affirmations because you'll be more likely to believe them!

This is the week where you can be more influenced by boys - so don't make any big decisions when it comes to the opposite sex. Wait a week or two to see if you still feel the same way when your hormones change again.

You'll be charismatic, using words like "I feel" and "I love," making it a great time for writing and creative activities.

As the week goes on, you might relax a bit, focusing less on tasks. Support ongoing projects and have fun—this phase is all about enjoying yourself!

# AUTUMN

*Creative Phase - Week 3 (Pre-Menstrual)*

After ovulation, estrogen drops a bit, but progesterone steps in to prevent a big dip. This means you won't feel as lively as in summer, and doubts may make you a bit moody.

It's a time to focus inward and take a break when needed.

You might feel more anxious and critical but remember it's temporary.

Learning and understanding new concepts can be more challenging, and you might find that you get more tongue-tied than normal.

This is a good time to do revision type work, or edit projects that you're working on.

On the upside, creative ideas may pop up. Grand ideas may come, but you'll find you won't have the energy to follow them through. Avoid pushing too hard physically.

You may feel drawn to declutter your personal space.

Look outward, skip overthinking, and embrace ease.

Power naps beat caffeine in this slow phase.

Watch for drama and communicate clearly; your mood swings will pass soon.

# WINTER

Your hormones, Estrogen and Progesterone, take a dip—it's like a roller coaster.

You might feel sad, irritable, tired, and find it hard to concentrate. It can be a tough time, like a stormy winter, and you will want to be alone, but people keep bothering you. Don't worry; spring is coming soon.

It's a great time to think deeply and figure out your purpose and dreams.

Activities that don't involve other people, that allow you to express yourself freely are great ways for you to 'positively escape'.

Take it easy, rest, and trust your instincts. Get more sleep if you need it; feeling a bit hazy is okay.

Slow down, go with the flow, and focus on what's important to you.

It's normal to feel a bit disconnected from other people.

Use this time to forgive and let go.

Embrace a peaceful mindset (the Red Flag exercise can be helpful during this week), take care of your body, and let your ego rest.

You're most accepting and present now (because you just couldn't be bothered with other people), so enjoy the moment and don't overthink.

# Honouring my Need for Rest and Alone Time

As you now know, the need for quiet time, a space to chill your thinking and just be is a natural part of your cycle as a female.

The mandalas in this journal give you the space to do just that.  Grab yourself your favourite colours, and when you need to quieten things, lose yourself in the simplicity of colouring

# Understanding my Female Brain & How it Plays Tricks Sometimes

When you experience things that cause you to emotionally react, jot your thoughts down here, and then revisit it a week or two later. Often our hormones cause us to blow things out of proportion, OR influence our feelings (in particular with relationships, or people we might feel attracted to).

By giving yourself the gift of TIME before acting on your feelings, you'll have more of an idea if how you feel is genuine, or if they've been exagerated by your hormones.

_____

_____

_____

_____

_____

_____

_____

_____

_____

_____

_____

_____

_____

_____

_____

_____

_____

_____

_____

_____

_____

# SECTION 4:
# TECHNIQUES FOR
# CHANGE

## Including "In-the-moment" techniques we call E.F.A. (Emotional First Aid)

Because life is full of ups and downs - we started this journal with empowering activities to elevate your ups, and give you those to reflect on when doubting your value, worth or uniqueness.

However, we have to be real too - and equip you with tools you can call on for when you're feeling down, that can help you see things in a better light, so you don't get too down, or feel you have no control over yourself.

The next 3 activities are great in-the-moment tools to call on to get you back into a good headspace quickly.

# E.F.A. Exercise 1 - RED-FLAG WORD EXERCISE

For Changing Negative Thinking

**PART 1**

Have you ever noticed that some words make you FEEL certain things?

Words like 'hurry' make you feel rushed. And 'STOP!' makes you pause and slow down.

There's a lot of words that cause us to have a physical and emotional reaction, and a lot of them are words that you use every single day, without even knowing how they make you feel.

There are also words that paint pictures in our head, that cause us to see the world a certain way.

When you are more aware of the words that you use, and the impact they have ON you, you are able to make different word choices that can have a great, positive impact on your day.

This next exercise is going to show you how to do that, by spending a few minutes a day getting real with yourself.

To start, you'll want to free-write your thoughts for no longer than 10 minutes on the next page, as soon as you wake up in the morning.

Write down everything that comes to your mind, without any filters or edits. Just let your thoughts flow naturally.

# The Thoughts I want to Change

Preparing for the Red Flag Word Exercise

I don't want to do go to work today. I should get up and get ready, but I feel so shit. I feel like I never say the right thing, I'm always being judged and I'm anxious all the time. I'm never enough.

# The Thoughts I want to Change

## Red Flag Word Exercise - Part 2

Now you've done that, go about your day as usual until you have a spare 15 minutes. During this time, take a look at the thoughts you wrote down earlier and identify any words that may be sabotaging or holding you back.

These words include BIG emotions, and any of the following:

| SABOTAGE WORD (red flags) | REPLACE WITH |
|---|---|
| • should | • Will (or want to) |
| • can't | • can |
| • but | • and |
| • don't | • do |
| • need | • want |
| • can't | • can |
| • won't | • will |
| • Greater | • Less |
| • hate | • love |
| • dislike | • like |
| • always | • never or rarely |
| • never | • often or always |
| • lazy | • energetic |
| • unworthy | • worthy |
| • never (always or sometimes) | • always (never or sometimes) |
| • sometimes | • often or never (whichever causes the least resistant feeling) |

You can use a red pen to cross out these words. Once you've identified the sabotage words, replace them with their opposite or with more compelling alternatives.

For example, if you come across a negative word, find a positive or empowering word to replace it with.

(example)

I don't want to do go to work today. I should get up and get ready, but I feel so shit. I feel like I never say the right thing, I'm always being judged and I'm anxious all the time. I'm never enough.

# The Thoughts I want to Change

## Red Flag Word Exercise - Part 3

Next, read the revised thoughts out loud to yourself and pay attention to how you feel.

You will notice a positive shift in your mindset and emotions and that's because we've changed the power behind the words!

It's important to make this exercise a regular practice, like a weekly "CHECK UP FROM THE NECK UP." You can even do it daily at first until it becomes a natural habit.

You can turn it into a fun game by challenging yourself to catch and replace those sabotaging words throughout the day.

If you slip up, the penalty can be saying the revised statement out loud in a more compelling way, wherever you are.

You can even involve your family to make it more enjoyable
(this is another way of making a difference to the people around you!)

Remember, the goal is to replace negative or sabotaging words with positive and empowering ones, and to create a more positive mindset.

Have fun with this exercise and enjoy the positive changes it can bring to your life!

# The Thoughts I want to Change
Use the Red Flag Word Exercise

# The Thoughts I want to Change
Use the Red Flag Word Exercise

# Beliefs I want to Change

Current Belief

eg: There's not enough money to go around

New Belief

eg: There's plenty f money to go around

# E.F.A. Exercise 2 -
# BALLOON POPPING EMOTIONS

## For Switching off Emotions to Think Straight

Sometimes life happens and our emotions can get the best of us. Life can be stressful, especially these days.

Emotionalising how we see ourselves, other people, the world and even the future is part of our design, and it's true that females in general feel emotions more intensely, more often; and it's completely normal.

The emotional brain (limbic system) in us with uterus-infused brains, is there to ensure bonding, whether we choose to become a mother, or not.

Consistent negative emotions can be a way to know we need to change something in our life and when we trust our intuition, they make a great life GPS system.

Still, in the moment, we often need to have our wits about us, so we can be more in control than most of us have been taught though, and this is powerful to discover, but it takes practice.

At these times, you are actually feeling them in a 'place' within your body, so you want to relocate them. As silly as it sounds, doing this sucks the momentary 'charge' out of it, which causes your frontal lobe 'lights' to come back on, so you can think straight, long enough to see more clearly, or get a break from the emotional 'pain'. It's possible when you get used to doing it.

To revisit any memory, we have to 'imagine' it as if it's happening again, and so if that's possible, so is manipulating any imagined events. Women join more dots between an event and arriving at its interpretation.

We can play out scenarios in our mind often, that cause us anxiety and stress, so here you can use this same natural power we each have, to take the 'charge' out of a situation, within just seconds.

If you think a stick is a snake on a walk, you release the same stress chemicals into your bloodstream as if it were real anyway, so if our mind can cause internal stress in how it 'see's things, we can use it's power to cause calm.

So we're going to use this Mind-Body connection to your advantage!

## BALLOON POPPING INSTRUCTIONS

Next time your emotions bring you down, or send you crazy, work yourself through this exercise.

1. Imagine the emotion is the air contained inside a balloon that is INSIDE of you.
2. Wherever in your body you feel that emotion, imagine that emotion is the air that is within a filled balloon right there.
3. Now you know what a balloon looks like full and also when it pops? It is just a bit of shrivelled up rubber, right?
4. NOW, imagine that you hold a big sharp needle and pop that emotion filled balloon, and then ask yourself:

'Now where has the emotion gone?' POP! Just like that, it is gone. Perhaps it ran out your toes and into the gutter down the street?

You'll notice the INTENSITY of the emotion you felt before has decreased, giving you more emotional freedom!

# E.F.A. Exercise 3 - 5 FINGER FLUSTER BUSTER

For When You're Flustered

This is a great tool with many benefits:

It helps us to become more positive, and less stressed.

It helps us to search for different meanings to situations and can really get our creative juices flowing in us.

It totally evolves our thinking to a new level of awareness and growth.

It helps us to make new choices, see options and ideas.

It helps us to take charge in the moment and over time, with practice, becomes an automatic response.

## INSTRUCTIONS:

**STEP 1** is your thumb = the TRIGGER (the event);

**STEP 2** is your pointer finger = the MEANING (you apply);

**STEP 3** is middle finger = the THOUGHTS (that follow the meaning);

**STEP 4** is your ring finger = the FEELINGS (that follow the thoughts);

**Step 5** is your little finger = the BEHAVIOUR (that follows the feelings).

# Photocopy and leave in the car

THE EVENT / TRIGGER: A car pulls out in front of you while driving to work

THE MEANING: The meaning you could give that event is likely to be a strong negative one.

THE THOUGHTS: The meaning you have applied causes you to THINK negative thoughts such as "That moron could have caused an accident"

THE FEELINGS: and that leads you to feel a certain way, probably anything but happy in this instance (eg, you start to doubt yourself); and

THE BEHAVIOUR: THAT causes you to behave in a way that likely leads to you lash out and lose your calm.

An alternative option could have been to apply a DIFFERENT meaning such as "I hope that person is not having a heart attack" or "I hope that person hasn't had bad news"

Can you see and feel the difference?

Which meaning will empower YOU to have the best and happiest day and not let it ruin your day?

# 30 Day Challenge - For Changing Habits

**New Habit:**

*eg. give someone a compliment, help someone, tell myself I'm good enough as I am, eat better food, talk to myself looking into my pupils not at my face to give a few ideas that make us better, meditate etc*

<u>**Why is this important for me?**</u>

<u>**Strengths:**</u>

<u>**Weaknesses:**</u>

**Reward:**

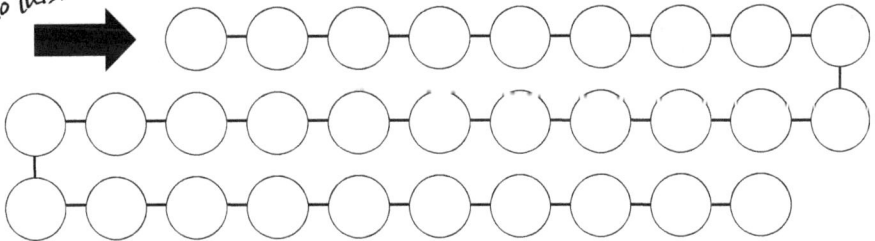

Let's do this!

<u>**How did it go?**</u>

<u>**What did I learn?**</u>

**Rate this challenge**

# 30 Day Challenge - For Changing Habits

**New Habit:**

_____

_____

_____

**Why is this important for me?**

_____

_____

_____

**Strengths:**

_____

**Weaknesses:**

_____

**Reward:**

_____

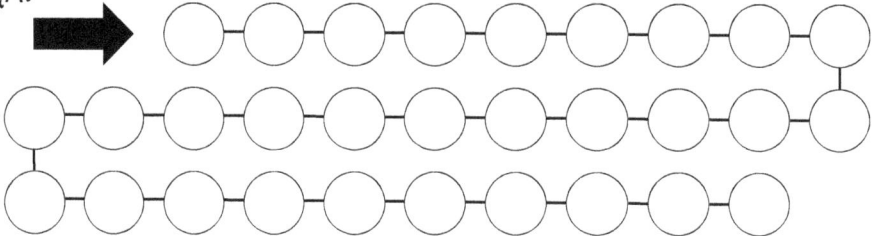

Let's do this!

**How did it go?**

_____

_____

_____

**What did I learn?**

_____

_____

_____

Rate this challenge

# 30 Day Challenge - For Changing Habits

New Habit:

Why is this important for me?

Strengths:

Weaknesses:

Reward:

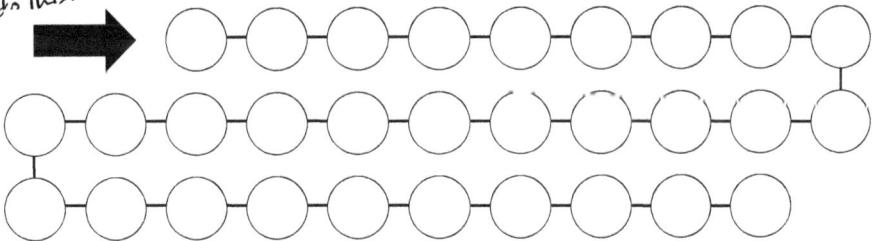

Let's do this!

How did it go?

What did I learn?

Rate this challenge

# 30 Day Challenge - For Changing Habits

**New Habit:**

**Why is this important for me?**

**Strengths:**

**Weaknesses:**

**Reward:**

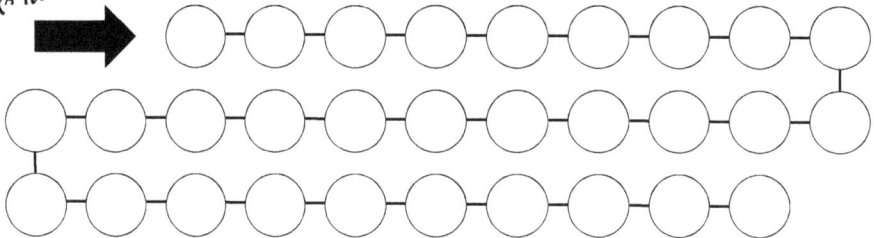

Let's do this!

**How did it go?**

**What did I learn?**

Rate this challenge ☆☆☆☆☆

# 30 Day Challenge - For Changing Habits

**New Habit:**

_____

_____

_____

**Why is this important for me?**

_____

_____

_____

**Strengths:**

_____

**Weaknesses:**

_____

**Reward:**

_____

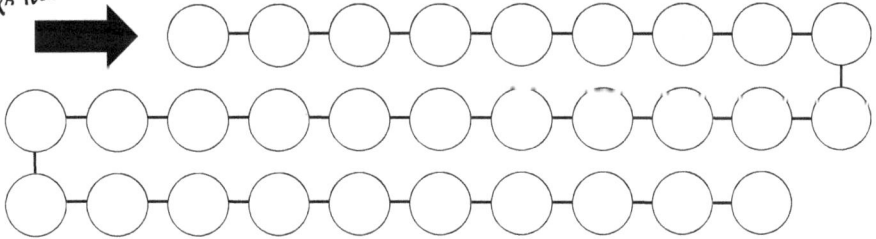

Let's do this!

**How did it go?**

_____

_____

_____

**What did I learn?**

_____

_____

_____

Rate this challenge

# 30 Day Challenge - For Changing Habits

**New Habit:**

_____

_____

_____

**Why is this important for me?**

_____

_____

_____

**Strengths:**

_____

**Weaknesses:**

_____

**Reward:**

_____

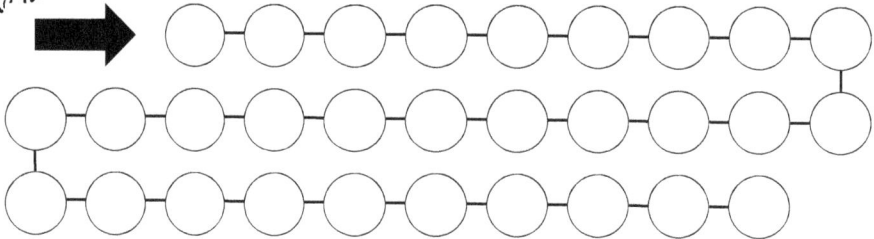

Let's do this!

**How did it go?**

_____

_____

_____

**What did I learn?**

_____

_____

_____

Rate this challenge

# 30 Day Challenge - For Changing Habits

**New Habit:**

_____

_____

_____

_____

**Why is this important for me?**

_____

_____

_____

_____

**Strengths:**

_____

_____

**Weaknesses:**

_____

_____

**Reward:**

_____

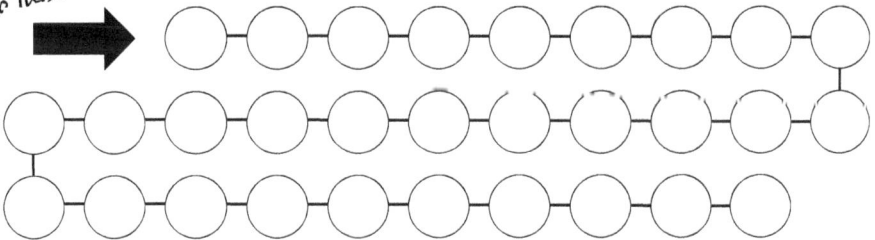

Let's do this!

**How did it go?**

_____

_____

_____

**What did I learn?**

_____

_____

_____

Rate this challenge

# Where to go for help, inspiration, motivation or guidance

Visit Her-Potentiality.Shop
To order your next journal, empowerment products,
resources and more.

Visit UnInstituteOfWomen.com
for the ultimate way to heal and empower women for a
living, fulfilment and a legacy.

Email admin@instituteofwomen.com
Let's empower women together, and become role models
of activated potentiality for girls and women. Let's send
the message that it's possible.

# The Issues I Want Gone for Good, and Need Help With

*For example; transfer Beliefs, Thoughts & Emotions from previous exercises to transform your life, fast, safely, profoundly, for good, with a qualified professional (Transformologist®) who can help you.*

*PS: If you don't have a Transformologist®, contact admin@instituteofwomen.com to get one*

*ISBN: 978-0-6486104-0-3*

*Amazing Media Productions Pty Ltd*
*PO Box 211*
*Buderim QLD 4556*

*Her-Potentiality.Shop*
*UnInstituteOfWomen.com*

www.ingramcontent.com/pod-product-compliance
Lightning Source LLC
Chambersburg PA
CBHW050634150426

42811CB00052B/805